Clara
Barton

by Jill C. Wheeler

visit us at
www.abdopub.com

Published by ABDO & Daughters, an imprint of ABDO
Publishing Company, 4940 Viking Drive, Suite 622, Edina,
Minnesota 55435. Copyright ©2002 by Abdo Consulting
Group, Inc. International copyrights reserved in all countries.
No part of this book may be reproduced in any form without
written permission from the publisher.

Printed in the United States.

Edited by Paul Joseph
Graphic Design: John Hamilton
Cover Design: Mighty Media
Interior Photos: Corbis and AP/Photo

Library of Congress Cataloging-in-Publication Data

Wheeler, Jill C., 1964-
    Clara Barton / Jill C. Wheeler
        p.   cm. -- (Breaking Barriers)
    Includes index.
    Summary: Examines the life of the nurse who served on the
battlefields of the Civil War and later founded the American Red
Cross.
    ISBN 1-57765-317-3
    1. Barton, Clara, 1821-1912--Juvenile literature. 2. Red Cross-
-United States--Biography--Juvenile literature. 3. Nurses--United
States--Biography--Juvenile literature. [1. Barton, Clara, 1821-1912.
2. Nurses. 3. Women--Biography. 4. American National Red
Cross.] I. Title.

    HV569.B3W52   2002
    361.7'634'092--dc21
    [B]

                                                    98-008334

Contents

A Beacon in the Storm

*S*eptember 11, 2001, started as a wonderful late-summer morning, with sunshine beaming through crystal blue skies. But those skies held a horror that turned the day into tragedy. At 8:45 a.m., a hijacked American Airlines jumbo jet slammed into the South Tower of New York's World Trade Center, engulfing the top floors in flames. At 9:03 a.m., another hijacked jet hit the North Tower. Many people fled to the streets below, but thousands more were trapped inside the burning buildings.

In Washington, D.C., at 9:38 a.m., terrorists controlling another hijacked plane crashed into the Pentagon, the center of America's military power. Hundreds were killed, and a whole section of the massive concrete building collapsed. Meanwhile, in rural Pennsylvania, yet another hijacked plane fell from the sky, killing all on board.

Back in New York City, the twin towers of the World Trade Center collapsed, causing even more destruction below. Thousands of people still trapped inside were killed. Hundreds of firefighters, police, and rescue workers also perished under the rubble.

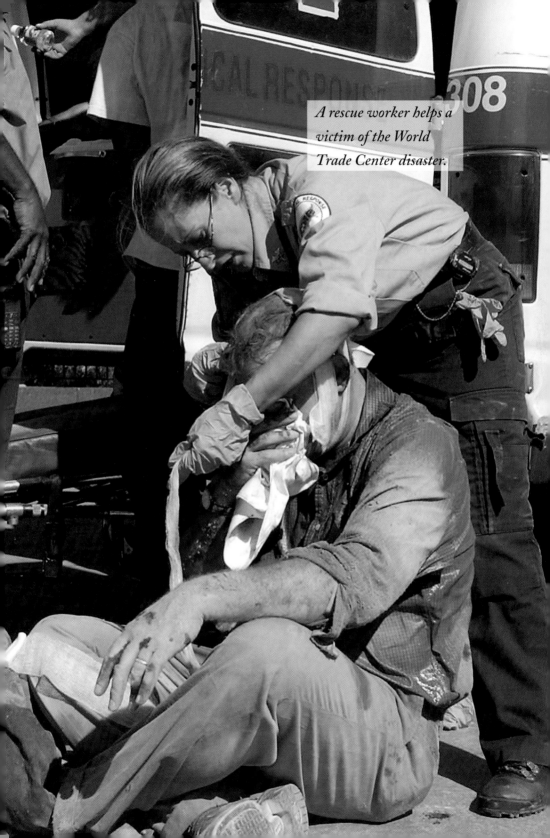

A rescue worker helps a victim of the World Trade Center disaster.

This was no "ordinary" disaster; it was a scene of unimagineable horror. But even before the worst was over, the American Red Cross sprang into action. All across the nation people donated blood, which the Red Cross rushed to New York. At the scene of the disaster itself, Red Cross volunteers helped thousands of victims obtain emergency food, clothing, and medicine. For the people of New York City, the Red Cross was one beacon of hope in a storm of darkness.

Today's American Red Cross has its roots in the accomplishments of one amazing woman who lived long ago. Like her modern counterparts, she believed her place was at the side of someone in need. This woman traveled the world, spreading hope and comfort in an era when women rarely went beyond the walls of their homes. This woman was named Clara Barton.

Clara Barton

From Shy Child to School Teacher

*C*larissa Harlowe Barton was born December 25, 1821, on a small farm near Oxford, Massachusetts. She was the youngest of five children. Her brothers, Stephen and David, and sisters, Sally and Dorothy, all were at least 10 years older. They and Clara's parents, Stephen and Sarah, all took charge of young Clarissa. "I had no playmates," Clara recalled, "but in effect six fathers and mothers."

Stephen Barton loved to tell his baby daughter stories, and she loved to listen. He told tales of his days when he was a soldier fighting Native Americans. In those days, the United States government frequently fought with Native Americans over land.

A small farm from the mid-1800's.

Clara delighted in asking him for more stories. "I learned that next to heaven, our highest duty was to love and serve our country," she said. She also learned about the life of a soldier. For example, she knew the difference between the cavalry (horse soldiers) and the infantry (foot soldiers). That knowledge would be a big help to her in the future.

Clara grew up a tomboy. She rode horses with her brothers and cousins and played other boyish games. She loved to play nurse. Her patients were pets that were sick or injured. Instead of staying inside and learning what young ladies were supposed to learn, she preferred being outdoors. Despite her activities, she was a very shy girl. Young Clara was so withdrawn that at times she couldn't even eat. It disturbed her parents greatly.

When Clara was 11, her brother David fell from the roof of a barn. The fall left him badly injured. He began a two-year recovery, during which his sister rarely left his side. She read to him, brought him food, and gave him his medicine. She even learned to apply leeches to his body. Leeches are parasitic worms that suck the blood out of their hosts. In those days, doctors believed leeches could help people feel better by sucking out sick blood.

When she was a child, Clara Barton loved to play nurse.

Schoolteachers of the mid-1800's.

When Clara was 16 years old, a family friend advised her to take up teaching. He thought it would help Clara overcome her shyness. At age 17, Clara did just that. She took a teaching position in her hometown. For the next 10 years she moved among the schools in the local district. It wasn't long before she gained a reputation as a strict disciplinarian. Even though she was only five feet (1.5 m) tall, she could handle even the biggest and toughest of students.

It was unusual in those days for a woman to have a career. It also was unusual for a woman to earn as much money as a man. Clara demanded both. "I may sometimes be willing to teach for nothing," she said. "But if paid at all, I shall never do a man's work for less than a man's pay."

Clara enjoyed teaching, yet she was always restless. She convinced her brothers to let her start a school for the children of their employees. She also helped out with church projects and distributed clothing to needy people. She kept her brothers' business records and learned to do complex calculations. Even that was not enough. Finally, she decided to go back to school. She enrolled at the Liberal Institute of Clinton, New York. There, she took every course she could. "I had the habit of study," she said, "with a burning anxiety to make the most of lost time."

Pioneer in Education

*C*lara's mother died while her daughter was in school. Clara was unable to make it home in time for the funeral. When she did return home, she realized things had changed. Clara was very sad, however, she no longer felt tied to her home.

Clara, now 30, and a friend headed for New Jersey. There, she took a job teaching in an exclusive private school. She liked the work but still felt a little restless. She often took walks after school. It was during those walks that she thought of her next challenge.

School was a privilege in Clara's day. Only children whose parents had money could get an education. Because of this, many children had nothing to do all day but work or get into trouble. Clara worried about the many young boys around town who had nowhere to go. She approached the local authorities with the idea of a school. They scoffed at her plan. Those children would be nothing but trouble, they told her. They didn't think Clara could handle such a task.

A young Clara Barton.

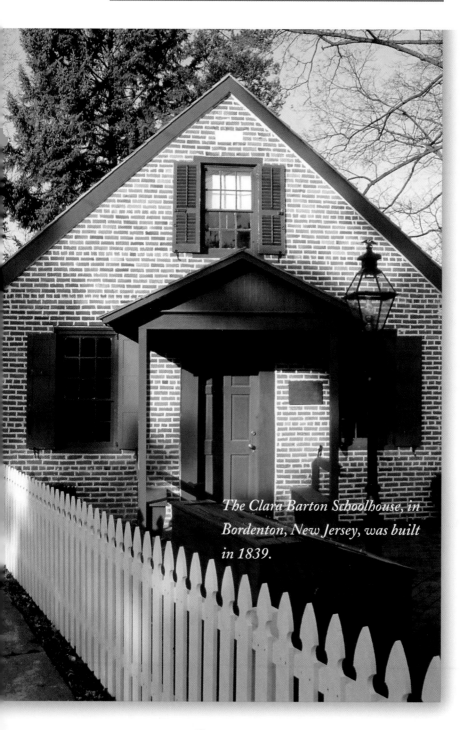

The Clara Barton Schoolhouse, in Bordenton, New Jersey, was built in 1839.

Clara didn't listen to them. She asked six of the local boys if they would like to go to school. They said yes, they would. Clara began to teach them for free. The next day, she had 20 students. Within a year, several hundred students had gathered at her school. Finally, the authorities had to give Clara a teacher's license and an old ramshackle school building.

Clara's school continued to grow. In less than three years it grew to more than 600 students. Some wealthy parents pulled their children out of private schools to attend. They liked the way Clara taught. Meanwhile, Clara had made history. She successfully had started the first free school in New Jersey.

Sadly, the authorities did not believe a woman could be in charge of such a large school. They appointed a man to be superintendent of the growing school. Clara was heartbroken. Her spirit temporarily broken, she began to lose her voice. With no voice, she couldn't teach. She resigned from the school and moved with a friend to Washington, D.C.

Battling Bureaucracy

*C*lara had decided an office job would give her vocal chords a welcome break. She took a job as a clerk in the United States Patent Office. This made her the first woman employee of the U.S. government.

Clara's job involved copying important documents by hand. Her bold, clear handwriting earned her 10 cents for each 100 words. Her boss, the Commissioner of Patents, quickly recognized that he could trust Clara. Eventually, she became his confidential clerk, at a salary of $1,400 per year. That was a large income for a woman in the 1850s.

Clara's success made some people nervous. In those days, many people believed men and women should not serve together in the workplace. Some men began trying to get Clara fired from her job. That made her all the more determined to succeed.

Clara would get to work by 9 A.M. and work until 3 P.M. Then she would take her work home with her and continue until midnight.

The U.S. Capitol under construction in 1860 in Washington, D.C.

She would be up early in the morning to do her housework and her shopping. She even would study French before it was time to work again.

Despite her extra effort, Clara lost her job when the political winds changed. She returned home in 1858 and spent two years nursing her eyes and her voice. She also nursed a hope that she could somehow rise above the lowly station that women had in those days.

After briefly considering a return to teaching, Clara moved back to Washington, D.C. Her friends at the Patent Office found more work for her. She also began socializing with many important people. She was invited to the inaugural ball for President Abraham Lincoln, but she could not attend because of a cold.

She, like many other people in the nation, sensed that a war between the states was coming. Clara was ready for it. "This conflict is one thing I've been waiting for," she said. "I'm well and strong and young— young enough to go to the front. If I can't be a soldier, I'll help soldiers."

A few months later, Confederate soldiers overtook a military outpost called Fort Sumter in Charleston, South Carolina. The prophecies had been right. The U.S. Civil War had begun.

Abraham Lincoln

War!

As soon as the war began, President Lincoln asked for 75,000 men to volunteer for the Union Army. That was what people called the Northern forces. The soldiers fighting for the South formed the Confederate Army.

Many men answered Lincoln's call, including a group from Massachusetts. They came to Washington, D.C., on their way to fight. Clara was eager to see them when she heard they were coming. Clara had taught many of the men in school. Now she sat and talked with them at their temporary quarters in the Senate chamber.

Clara enjoyed talking to these old friends. Yet she was upset by their lack of supplies for war. She quickly rummaged through her house, tearing up old sheets for towels and handkerchiefs. She wrote to the families of the soldiers back in Massachusetts and begged them to send supplies. The soldiers needed everything from food to blankets and candles. The donations poured in. Clara's home began to look like a warehouse.

Union soldiers in the trenches before the Battle of Petersburg.

Confederate dead lie in a trench at the Battle of Fredericksburg, Virginia.

As the war progressed, Clara realized many soldiers were dying unnecessarily. They would be wounded in battle, then transported to Washington, D.C., for treatment. Many did not survive the trip. Clara decided the Army Medical Department needed to do more for the soldiers on the battlefield. She had definite ideas on what needed to be done.

It took Clara more than a year to get permission from the Army to put her plan into action. Thanks to her Washington friends, she finally received permission to take her supplies right to the battlefield. It was a dangerous plan, but to Clara, it was the only choice. "What could I do but go with them?" she said of the soldiers. "Or work for them and my country? The patriot blood of my father was warm in my veins."

In August 1862, Clara set out with a wagon of nursing supplies. "When our armies fought on Cedar Mountain, I broke the shackles and went to the field," she wrote in her journal. "And so began my work."

She arrived at midnight, two days after the battle. The field hospital was out of dressings for wounds. Brigade Surgeon James Dunn was astounded to see Clara and her wagon. "I thought that night if heaven ever sent out a holy angel, she must be one," he said. From then on, Clara became the "Angel of the Battlefield."

Angel of the Battlefield

*T*he Civil War was among the bloodiest conflicts in U.S. history. Soldiers fought with muskets, cannons, and bayonets. Wounded soldiers frequently were left on the battlefield to suffer and die slowly. There were not enough doctors and nurses to help them. Those who got help often faced having their wounded limbs amputated.

Clara vowed to do whatever she could for the suffering soldiers. She brought them wine, water, or whatever food she had. She would bandage their wounds or help a doctor operate on them. She would write letters from them to send to loved ones. Once, she removed a bullet from a soldier's jaw with her pocketknife. Sometimes, she just held their hands as they died.

Clara's work soon became legendary. The Army doctors did not want her around at first. Then they realized what a help she was. She had a talent for showing up just when they needed her, with the right supplies.

Clara Barton helps a wounded Civil War soldier.

A rare photo of a Civil War surgeon at work.

Clara would load train cars with her supplies and send them to Fairfax Station in Manassas, Virginia. The station also served as a center for emergency treatment and transportation of wounded soldiers to Alexandria, Virginia.

One of the bloodiest battles of the Civil War was the Second Battle of Bull Run. Clara heard about the battle while in Washington, D.C. She raced to Fairfax Station with supplies and several other women to help her. The wounded from Bull Run were being brought there by the wagonload. Clara stepped off the train to find the local woods covered with soldiers. She wrote in her journal that the "whole hillside seemed to be covered with bloody men."

Clara worked throughout the night to help more than 3,000 wounded men. She gave them water and food by candlelight. The men were so close together it was hard to avoid stepping on them. "The slightest misstep brought a torrent of groans," she wrote. From Saturday to Monday, she barely slept or ate.

Bull Run turned into the Battle of Chantilly. The Army brought in more soldiers who needed care. By now, Clara was working alone. Her helpers were too exhausted to continue. To make matters worse, the Confederate forces were advancing on the station.

Yet Clara worked up until the end. She caught the last train out before Confederate soldiers burned the train station to the ground. On her return to Washington, D.C., she slept for 24 hours.

In September 1862, Clara got word of another battle in Maryland in a place called Antietam. She loaded her wagon with supplies and joined the long line of Army wagons headed for battle. Yet her wagon was near the end of the chain. Clara urged her drivers to step out of line and drive all night to get there faster.

Antietam was the single bloodiest day in the entire war. Surgeons already had run out of dressings when Clara arrived. They were using cornhusks to staunch the flow of blood from wounds.

Clara began to work immediately. Bullets whizzed over her head as she brought food and water to wounded soldiers. Once, Clara was giving a wounded man a drink of water. She felt a ripple in the sleeve of her dress, and realized a bullet had ripped through it. Sadly, the bullet struck and killed the soldier she was helping. Clara continued working nonstop until dark. After dark, she brought lanterns from her supplies so the grateful surgeons could continue working.

Clara had another close call after the Battle of Fredericksburg, Virginia, in December 1862. She was

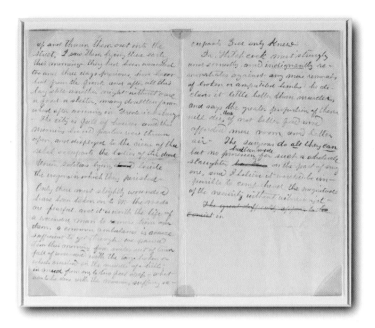

Clara Barton's handwritten notes on the Battle of Fredericksburg are now stored in the Library of Congress, in Washington, D.C.

hurrying to aid a surgeon who had asked for her help on the front lines. As she crossed a swaying bridge across the Rappahannock River, a soldier reached out to give her a hand. "While our hands were raised, a piece of an exploding shell hissed through between us," she said. The shell tore through part of her dress and part of the soldier's coat. Clara made it safely to help the doctor, but the gallant soldier who had helped her was carried in minutes later. He was dead.

Clara always was resourceful. Once, Army officers feared they had no more food, until Clara came to the rescue. She had brought cases of wine to help ease the soldiers' pain. Instead of being packed in sawdust as usual, some of the wine was packed in cornmeal. Clara immediately made cornmeal gruel to feed the soldiers.

Throughout the war, Clara continued to nurse soldiers, and gather and transport critical supplies to the battlefield. Her supplies always arrived before the Army's. The Army had to wait until the battle was over before sending help. That way, they didn't risk their precious supplies falling into enemy hands.

It was very dangerous for Clara to come to the front lines while the battle still raged. Yet she felt it was better that way. "I could run the risk," she said. "It made no difference to anyone if I were shot or taken prisoner; and I tried to fill that gap."

*Clara Barton risked her
life to help Civil War
soldiers on the battlefield.*

Army Nurse

*B*y 1863, the Army Medical Department was prepared to fight a major war. Clara's services were no longer as necessary. The Army even had a 500-nurse corp called the U.S. Sanitary Commission. Rather than joining that group, Clara chose to remain independent.

She spent eight months in Hilton Head, South Carolina, nursing soldiers wounded in and around Charleston. In May 1864, she returned to Washington to help victims of battles farther north. Outside town, a rain had turned the road into a river of mud, miring wagonloads of wounded. Clara waded through mud up to her knees, giving crackers to the starving soldiers.

Late in the war, the Army invited Clara to become supervisor of nurses for the Union Army. Now she worked in a hospital instead of on the battlefield. She had some 1,200 soldiers to nurse and feed. She wrote to her family about dealing with 700 loaves of bread for breakfast, 170 gallons (644 liters) of coffee, 200 gallons (757 liters) of soup, and 500 slices of buttered toast.

A photo of Clara Barton taken in 1865, near the end of the Civil War.

Tireless to the end, Clara remained at the hospital as the war wound down. She also decided that her next job should be to help the families of missing Union soldiers get information about their loved ones. Clara's unique work on the battlefields made her a perfect choice for the job. She devised a plan and asked a friend to present it to President Abraham Lincoln.

Clara Barton helped thousands of families find information about their missing loved ones after the Civil War.

In March 1865, she received a letter from President Lincoln. He approved of her plan and asked the Army to help her. Clara had no idea what she was in for. As she began her job, she realized that the Army had little information that could help her. Nearly 359,000 Union soldiers had died in the war. Only 172,000 of their graves were marked.

Clara compiled a list of the missing soldiers' names. It was so long she had to get the government to help her print it. Once the list was printed, she published the names in local newspapers. Other soldiers wrote to tell her what had happened to many of those men. Some men who were safe and sound at home wrote that their names were on the list. Others who had seen comrades die told her who they were, and when and how they died. These efforts helped Clara bring information to some 22,000 families of soldiers.

During this time, a young soldier from Connecticut approached Clara. He had been a prisoner of war at the Andersonville Prison Camp in Georgia. There, the Confederacy had confined captured Union soldiers. More than 13,000 Union prisoners of war had died there during the war. Confederate soldiers buried their bodies in unmarked graves. The soldier who contacted Clara thought he could identify many of the dead soldiers. He asked Clara to help. Together, they identified all but 440 of the dead. Andersonville is now a national cemetery.

Andersonville Prison during the Civil War.

The Andersonville Prison cemetery is the final resting place of thousands of Union soldiers.

Picking Up the Pieces

*T*he end of the Civil War left the United States in a shambles. It also left Clara Barton wondering what her next crusade would be. She decided to become a lecturer telling about the war. In 1866, she began traveling from town to town to speak. Thousands of people crammed into auditoriums to hear the woman everyone knew as the Angel of the Battlefield. In the meantime, she kept working to find missing soldiers.

The speaking engagements took a toll on Clara, who was nearly 48 years old. Her doctors ordered her to take a rest. She set sail for Europe in 1869 to take an overdue and much deserved vacation.

Clara still had not recovered her health when war broke out between France and Prussia (now part of Germany) in the summer of 1870. Yet she raced off to the battlefields there to do whatever she could.

Clara used her skills and her connections to raise money for refugees and set up hospitals. Many of the desperately poor refugees were in danger of dying— not from bullets, but from disease and unsanitary living conditions. Clara's work with them and on the battlefield earned her the thanks of several European governments.

Refugees from the Franco-Prussian War.

A New Crusade

*W*hile in Europe, Clara learned of an international organization called the Red Cross. The idea for the group came from Swiss businessman Henri Dunant. Like Clara, Dunant had helped soldiers on the battlefield. He had seen the miserable conditions in which they suffered. He worked to form an organization that would aid all wounded soldiers in times of war.

The Red Cross was formed at the Geneva Convention of 1864. That was when a group of nations got together to discuss how war could be made more humane. One of their suggestions was to start the Red Cross. Its purpose was to provide wartime help to soldiers, prisoners of war, and civilians who were wounded or sick.

Clara saw the Red Cross at work during the Franco-Prussian War. She found herself volunteering with them to help. Their organization and efficiency impressed her. "No needless suffering, no starving, no lack of care," she said of their efforts. "I said to myself, 'If I live to return to my country, I will try to make my people understand the Red Cross and that treaty.'"

Clara did return to the United States in 1873. She still had not recovered her health, so she settled in quiet Danville, New York. While recovering, she remembered her pledge. Clara always had been a person who needed a purpose. Now, she had a new one.

For seven years, Clara worked to promote the Red Cross in the United States. She published a booklet to educate Americans about the Red Cross.

Barton receives the work of Jean-Henri Dunant, her inspiration for the American Red Cross.

Clara Barton

Clara also suggested that the organization provide help to victims of natural disasters in peacetime. She wrote to members of Congress and asked for their help. She met with three different presidents. In 1877, International Red Cross authorities officially invited Clara to establish an American part of the organization.

On May 21, 1881, Clara and 22 supporters met with Michigan Senator Omar Congden to form the American Association of the Red Cross. Then, in 1882, the United States Senate ratified the Geneva Convention. The convention included the International Red Cross. Clara was elected the first president of the organization. She was 60 years old.

New Battlefields

*T*he United States now was at peace, but the Red Cross still had much work to do. Local Red Cross chapters began to spring up across the country. All had to raise their own funds from donations. In the fall of 1881, a series of devastating forest fires swept through Michigan. "There is no food left in its (the fire's) track for a rabbit to eat and, indeed, no rabbit to eat it," Clara said. Local Red Cross chapters raised an astonishing $80,000 to help with relief efforts.

The 1880s saw no more war, but plenty of natural disasters. Both the Mississippi and Ohio Rivers experienced severe flooding. Charleston, South Carolina, shook under an earthquake. A tornado tore through Mount Vernon, Illinois. Each time, Clara and her Red Cross volunteers were there to help. They brought with them clothing, food, supplies, medicine, and shelter. Most of all, they brought caring and hope.

Once again, the nation took note of this trail-blazing woman. After the horrendous Johnstown Flood of 1889, the local newspaper wrote a tribute to Clara. "How shall we thank Miss Clara Barton and the Red Cross for the help they have given us?" the paper said. "It cannot be done… We cannot describe the sunshine… Words fail."

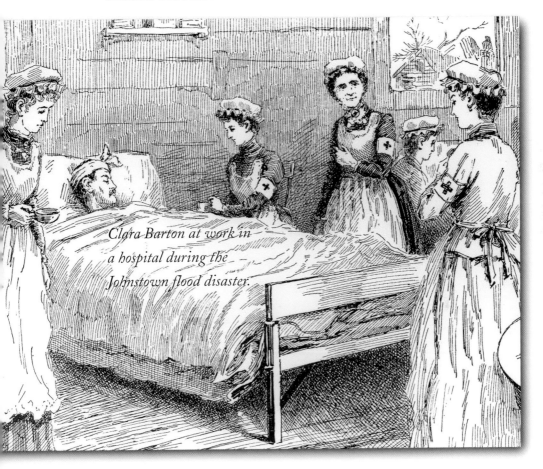

Clara Barton at work in a hospital during the Johnstown flood disaster.

There was always plenty of work for Red Cross volunteers in the United States. Yet when people needed help overseas, they were quick to respond. The American Red Cross donated grain to Russia after a crop failure there in 1892. Clara later traveled to Armenia to help victims of a religious war.

She also traveled to Cuba during its war of independence from Spain. She was in Havana when the U.S.S. *Maine* mysteriously exploded in Havana Harbor. That tragedy brought the United States into the war against Spain. The Red Cross went to work again, this time its first official wartime assignment. Clara oversaw aid to wounded soldiers in Cuba.

By 1902, Clara Barton's name was a household word in the United States. Many people around the world also knew of her. It was no surprise that the International Red Cross invited Clara to their conference in St. Petersburg, Russia, that year. She was to be the special guest of the Czar of Russia.

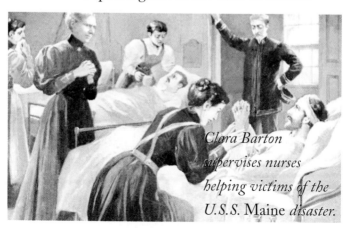

Clara Barton supervises nurses helping victims of the U.S.S. Maine *disaster.*

Clara Barton with a former slave child.

Retirement at Last

*C*lara was 80 years old when she returned from Russia. As she sailed across the ocean back to the U.S., she faced an uncertain future. She knew she had many critics within the American Red Cross. They complained that she was too old. They said she was not doing a good job of running the organization. Some claimed she was simply too old to do the job.

The Red Cross ran very differently than Clara was used to. During the Civil War, she had done whatever she needed to do to get the job done. Most of the time, she didn't bother asking permission. She just acted fast. The Red Cross charter didn't work that way. It demanded accountability. To get permission required time and special procedures.

Political fights within the Red Cross forced Clara to resign as president in 1904. This turn of events hurt her deeply. For a while, she struggled with depression. Yet later in the year, she bounced back. She had settled into her home in Glen Echo, Maryland, to enjoy her retirement.

Personal items from the Clara Barton Museum.

Reporters still sought out Clara for her opinion on everything from war to current court cases. She read many magazines and newspapers to keep up with world events. She closely followed the crusade to get women the right to vote. One of the leading proponents of women's suffrage had been Susan B. Anthony. She had been a friend of Clara's.

Clara Barton (second from left) with friends on the front porch of her home at Glen Echo, Maryland.

Susan B. Anthony

A Living Memorial

*C*lara Barton led a remarkable life and saw more than most women of that time. "What armies and how much of war I have seen," she wrote in her journal. "What thousands of marching troops, what fields of slain, what prisons, what hospitals... And yet one lives and laughs as if nothing had happened and thanks good fortune that it is as well as it is."

Clara died at her home on April 12, 1912. She was 90 years old. Newspapers around the world carried news of the death of the Angel of the Battlefield. The Red Cross and White House were strangely silent on the matter.

Yet a simple event following her funeral underscored her impact on the world. Clara's family was moving her body to Massachusetts for burial when a thick fog hampered their efforts. The ferry they wanted was not running, so they hired a private wagon.

Clara Barton

When the wagon driver learned he was carrying the body of Clara Barton he dropped his reins. He told Clara's family that his father had been a Confederate soldier at the battle of Antietam. He was wounded in the neck and was bleeding to death when Clara found him. The driver told Clara's family she had bound his father's wounds—and saved his life.

Clara Barton's vision of humanitarian aid lives on today in the American Red Cross. Likewise, their motto is one Clara herself would have approved: Help Can't Wait.

A Red Cross supply truck helps disaster victims.

Together...

We Send Hope and Help Around the World

The American Red Cross works tirelessly with its Red Cross partners worldwide to relieve human suffering and empower the most vulnerable to better help themselves in the future.

International Services

For those who wish to support the American Red Cross worldwide humanitarian programs, contributions can be made to the American Red Cross International Response Fund, P.O. Box 37243, Washington, DC 20013 or by calling 1-800-HELP-NOW or 1-800-257-7575 (Spanish).

The Red Cross continues to help victims of war and disasters throughout the world. This poster shows a young refugee in Kosovo receiving food from a Red Cross station.

Wounded soldiers rest at a Civil War hospital. Clara Barton helped to improve conditions for the sick and injured.

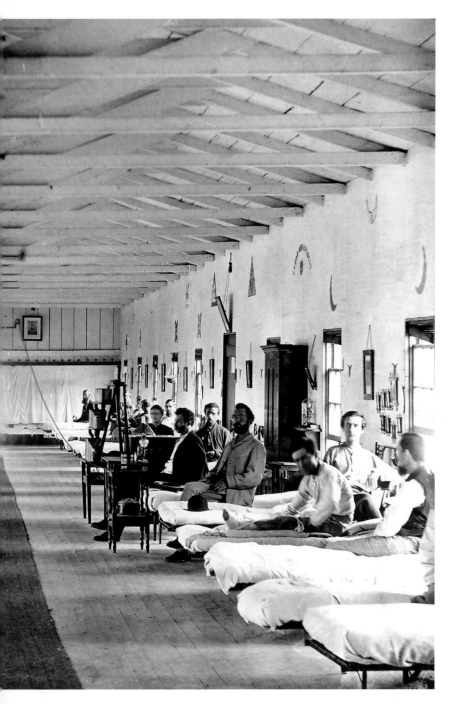

Timeline

December 25, 1821: Clara Barton born on a small farm near Oxford, MA.

1838: Becomes a school teacher.

1865: Assigned by President Lincoln the task of identifying missing Civil War soldiers. Between 1865 and 1868 she trackes down more than 22,000 missing soldiers.

1869: Travels to Europe. Learns about the Geneva Convention and the Red Cross. Joins the Red Cross and helps out during the Franco-Prussian War.

1877: Returns to the United States. Educates public and politicians about the Red Cross.

1881: American Red Cross established. Clara Barton elected president, a post she holds for over two decades.

1889: Led the Red Cross in its first major disaster relief effort after the Johnstown flood in Pennsylvania.

1904: Resigns from the Red Cross and retires to her home in Glen Echo, NY.

April 12, 1912: Clara Barton dies at age 90.

Where on the Web?

http://www.incwell.com/Biographies/Barton.html

Clara Barton, a Spectrum biography.

http://www.nps.gov/clba/

Clara Barton National Historic Site, featuring Clara Barton's house in Glen Echo, Maryland.

http://lcweb.loc.gov/exhibits/treasures/trm072.html

Documents and photos of Clara Barton, from the American Treasures collection of the United States Library of Congress.

http://www.redcross.org/

Web site of the American Red Cross.

http://www.cr.nps.gov/seac/andearch.htm

Information on the Civil War's Andersonville Prison camp, from the National Park Service.

Glossary

cavalry
Soldiers trained to fight on horseback.

Geneva Convention
An international agreement signed in Geneva, Switzerland, in 1864. The Geneva Convention created a code for the care and treatment of wartime sick, wounded, dead, and of prisoners of war. It also includes protection of civilians and hospitals displaying the symbol of the Red Cross.

gruel
Thin, watery porridge.

infantry
Soldiers trained to fight on foot.

musket
A type of gun that shoots lead balls.

Red Cross
An organization that provides help during natural disasters and during times of war.

refugees
People who must flee their homes because of war or a natural disaster.

women's suffrage
The right of women to vote.

Clara Barton

Index